AF866686

Drawings in the Palm of Your Hand

New Power and Freedom for Creative Professionals

Gordon B. Arnold AIA

Copyright © 2011 by Gordon B. Arnold, All Rights Reserved

No part of this publication may be reproduced, stored in a retrieval system, or transmitted in any form or by any means, electronic, mechanical, photocopying, recording, scanning, or otherwise, except as permitted under Section 107 or 108 of the 1976 United States Copyright Act, without the prior written permission of the Publisher.

ISBN-13: 978-0615517537

ISBN-10: 0615517536

By Gordon B. Arnold AIA

(817)233-4906

Email: garnold@citygraphs.com

To my wonderful wife Gail,

whose support and encouragement

makes this a wonderful life.

Foreword

In the summer of 2009, my wife asked me what I wanted for my birthday. At that time the new iPhone was a hot item and my old cell phone was past retirement. So, I took a leap of faith, never having used an Apple product, and said, "I'd like an iPhone." When the new iPhone 3G arrived at my local Apple Retail Store, I was one of the crazy people standing in line, ready to buy. After getting it home and experimenting with it, I discovered something amazing: I could call up a floor plan on the screen, pan around the image by sliding my finger across the surface and zoom in and out by "pinching" with my thumb and forefinger! So it occurred to me, if I could do that with a single drawing, then it was now possible to carry around a complete set of drawings for a construction project in my pocket!

For a while I had known it was time to leave my position with a local architectural firm. But then what? Now, all of a sudden, the direction ahead was clear. I could use my thirty five years of experience with producing construction projects to answer the question: If we can carry around a set of drawings on our handheld devices, what do we do with them once we get them to the screen? The answer was obvious:

We deal with them as construction professionals do. We sketch on them, we place notes on them, we create punch lists that are tied to them and we perform site studies before producing them – and we perform these tasks with easy-to-use, inexpensive applications. I decided it was time to use my project management skills to produce applications for other construction professionals. Now after having devoted two years to applications development, I believe other creative professionals can do the same. This book will show you how.

I write from the standpoint of an architect, but I hope readers will find the concepts discussed applicable to other fields. This is not a technical manual on the operation of smartphones and tablets. I assume the reader is familiar with managing images on these devices, and I occasionally refer to various resources and applications currently on the market that I've found helpful. This book covers, instead, how we can apply the power of these devices to the business of creating projects, getting them built, and even using our experience with the process to create digital tools for others.

Each chapter begins with a screen shot of an iPhone application. All of them are examples of the apps I have developed. They also are examples of the variety of applications that we can tailor to the way we work. These apps are easy to use, inexpensive, and readily available. They are the kinds of tools you can use to be more productive and produce for your clients.

List of Illustrations

iPhone screen showing interface for uScaleit+ app 1

iPhone screen showing area outline produced by uScaleit+ app 13

iPad screen showing Photo Albums thumbnails of architectural drawings 24

iPad screen showing list of architectural drawings in Dropbox app 24

iPhone screen showing result of area calculation produced by uScaleit+ app 25

iPhone screen showing virtual pen sketch produced by uSketchit+ app 33

iPhone screen showing sketch produced by uSketchit+ app 45

iPhone screen showing drawing with notes produced by uCantMeanIt app 51

iPhone screen showing photograph with notes produced by uCantMeanIt app 63

icon for uScaleit+ application 65

icon for uSketchit+ application 67

icon for uCantMeanIt application..............................69

icon for uPunchit+ application....................................71

iPhone screen showing aerial photograph with notes produced by uCantMeanIt app...........................77

iPhone screen showing floor plan with numbers and clouds produced by uPunchit+ app 83

iPad screen showing SketchUp model in iTeleport ...89

iPhone screen showing list of notes produced by uPunchit+ app...97

Table of Contents

I. Toward an Architecture of Digital Mobility.......... 1

Where Is the Construction Industry Going?......... 3

Enter the Smartphone Industry 5

The Smartphone Is Just the Beginning 7

Smartphone or Tablet? 9

A Match That Was Meant to Be 11

II. Consolidation, Communication and Collaboration.. 13

Synchronization 14

Construction in the "Cloud" 18

Teams Are Getting Bigger 20

How Project Documentation Might Evolve....... 22

III. The Internet and Spheres of Influence............... 25

Thinking Globally 26

Finding Your Global Team 27

Concept Communication with Pictures........... 31

IV. Mobile Drawings and Specifications 33
Impact on the Construction Industry 34
Mobile Drawing Management 35
Document Presentation and Management..... 39
The Changing Scenario 41
Return on Investment... 42

V. Diversifying the Company 45
New Products and Services 46
The Global Marketplace 48

VI. Producing an Application 51
The Essence of Application Development........ 52
Lessons Learned 54

VII. The Citygraphs Applications 63
uScaleit+ 65
uSketchit+ 67
uCantMeanIt 69
uPunchit+ 71
Other Apps for Design and Construction 73

VIII. Producing a Project Manual as an eBook 77

Another New Skill 78

Impact on the Process 80

IX. The Future of the Industry 83

Changes in the Construction Industry 84

Construction in the Twenty-First Century 85

Design Flow 90

New Expectations 91

"Bottling" and Exporting Experience 94

About the Author 97

Index 99

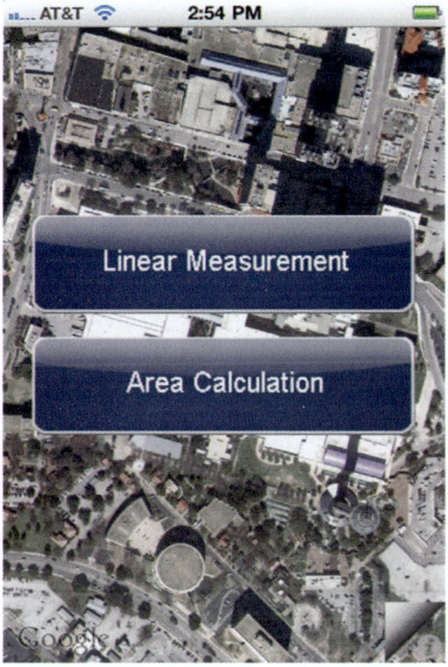

I.
Toward an Architecture of Digital Mobility

Two seemingly disconnected industries are about to become inextricably linked. The construction industry – home to concrete trucks, hardhats and job shacks has embraced the smartphone industry – the domain of high-tech applications, computer geeks, and Silicon Valley. Construction projects may seem at first glance to run on manual labor, and materials like concrete, steel and wood. But before any of those things come into play, the construction industry runs primarily on one thing: the flow of information.

Information flow makes raw materials flow. Everything needs to be documented via detailed construction drawings, shop drawings, specifications, ASI's, and RFI's, along with seemingly endless revisions. There are bills of materials, construction estimates, construction schedules, and their attendant revisions. Punch lists and meeting notes, many hand-written, pile up in that job shack where they can be hard to find, hard to edit, and hard to share.

Smartphones and tablets have revolutionized the storage, presentation, and sharing of this information. And yet, within the design and construction professions, paper drawings remain the most important component of the entire process. Creative people and builders, in any industry, still communicate with pictures, just as they always have. Despite technological advances, drawings still describe the quantity and location of materials, and specifications describe quality. What is most important now, however, is that our new storage, presentation and sharing tools let us manage, display, and "markup" drawings when they are in the right file format, just like a photograph on hand held devices. And just as we share pictures of our children, our pets, and our vacations, so too can we share architectural drawings and other relevant images that are essential to the business of producing projects. Once we realize this, we can leverage our smartphones, tablets and the endless numbers of applications that run on them to display, edit, manage, and share these important images.

It is now possible to carry around a complete set of construction drawings and specifications for a project on a handheld device, saving all of the energy and time that has for so long been associated with producing multiple sets of paper documents.

▶ Where Is the Construction Industry Going? ◀

Some say the domestic construction industry's best days are behind it. The United States will probably not see a resurgence of the post-war construction booms of the 1950s. Globally, however, construction growth has barely begun, as emerging economies build out their infrastructures. India, China, and Brazil today are where the United States was in the 1950s. A country's GDP today seems to be the inverse of the growth in its construction industry. While India rapidly develops roads, and China erects factories and housing, the U.S. construction industry focuses more on upgrading and retrofitting. The recession that started in 2007, and the housing and credit crises that followed, have all converged to drive down demand for new construction in this country.

What does this mean for the construction industry and design professionals? It means that our industry has matured and is entering a new phase. Increased profits for design and construction firms will not be achieved simply with organic growth, but through consolidation, communication, and collaboration. None of these developments may seem to have much to do with smartphones and tablets, but changes in the construction industry will increasingly be influenced by the mobility, immediacy, and convenience of these devices

First, consolidation in the construction industry will come through companies merging to achieve growth. As a result, a construction company may have multiple offices, with divisions in New York, Chicago, London, Bangkok, Bangalore and beyond. Engineers, architects, and project managers will move between offices frequently. Personnel in multiple cities will be working together on a single project, creating the need for greater communication and better data sharing. The mobile quality of smartphones and tablets for design and construction professionals will support this development.

"Doing more with less" - being efficient - is the mantra of business in the twenty first century, and the construction industry is no exception. Another way to improve the bottom line is to simply make operations more efficient with better communication. Today, that's done with modern technology. Making the most of easy-to-use, inexpensive, and readily available technology, like smartphones and tablets, and their applications, can speed up the process of solving problems. That means freeing people to do more and share their information quickly.

Finally, collaborating or "partnering" with people and organizations beyond our immediate sphere of influence makes more sense than hiring more staff. Collaborating with design and construction professionals on the other side of the world is now possible but comes at a price. We must be more accessible wherever we are, even in different time zones. Mobile devices are just the tools to keep us in touch with one another.

▶ Enter the Smartphone Industry ◀

A completely separate industry, a product of Silicon Valley innovation, has changed the way people communicate with each other. Smartphones are a "disruptive" technology. They have dramatically changed how we communicate, work, and play.

Smartphones have evolved over the years, but what has really changed the dynamic is touchscreen technology and "gestures." The ability to launch applications by touching an icon on the screen, pan around an image on the screen by dragging your finger, or zoom in and out of it by "pinching" or spreading your fingers has made the user experience fun and easy. In addition, smartphones are taking on more power and features and they are contributing to an interesting convergence in the industry. While smartphones are becoming more feature-rich, computers are becoming smaller. Inevitably, the smartphone will one day become a full-featured, pocket-sized computer, with the same applications, features, and storage capacity as a current laptop.

As this trend continues, the smartphone and the tablet will become less of a casual curiosity and more of a valuable, productive business tool for all industries. The software industry has responded with a host of SaaS (software-as-a-service) applications designed specifically for the smartphone. SaaS applications and data are hosted remotely and accessed as needed from a mobile device. Customer resource management (CRM) applications are already available, giving mobile staff members easy access to customer data while on the road. Project management tools, contact managers, and other business-critical functions are readily available on all major smartphone platforms. The construction industry has started to notice.

Smartphones and tablets are evolving before our eyes from being entertaining consumer devices to valuable tools that perform useful tasks. They are helping design and construction professionals consolidate their resources, increase efficiency via immediate communication, and collaborate with ease.

▶ The Smartphone Is Just the Beginning ◀

We tend to think of the iPhone when we think of smartphones simply because that particular device is the most popular in the consumer world. Apple has created a popular platform that is attractive and fun to use. It also has a wealth of both consumer and business applications. But do you need an iPhone to take advantage of this new way of doing business? Not really.

Apple's iOS is only one of a number of platforms for smartphones. According to Gartner (February 2011), worldwide smartphone sales by operating system in 2010 were as follows: Symbian at 37.6 percent, Android at 22.7 percent, Research In Motion at 16 percent, Apple iOS at 15.7 percent, Microsoft at 4.2 percent and Others at 3.8 percent.

As Drew Crawford, a busy app developer put it:

"Android, on the other hand, is accelerating pretty quickly and by many metrics will probably overtake iOS as a platform. On the other hand, it is very fragmented, with lots of software working only on a subset of Android devices. So from a software developer's perspective, it isn't really clear to what extent it should be considered a single platform, and to what extent it's really a set of related platforms. In either case, there's a great deal of uncertainty about which platform makes the best long-term strategy for software developers."

It is next to impossible to keep up with the new devices and operating system features that are appearing every day but thanks to all of this innovation, we do have choices.

The *Wall Street Journal* recently stated the following:

"While personal computers are not going to disappear altogether, the trend lines are clear. Gartner, the market research company, predicts that by 2013 the number of smartphones will surpass PCs, 1.82 billion to 1.78 billion. And that's not counting the tablets. Gene Munster, an analyst with the global investment bank Piper Jaffray, estimates that Apple iPad sales were 14.5 million for 2010, with another million tablets sold by competitors. Sarah Rotman Epps at Forrester Research predicts that 82 million Americans will be using tablets by 2015."

▶ Smartphone or Tablet? ◀

Smartphones are enormously popular, and chances are, most construction professionals have one. The big advantage of the smartphone is that it is a crossover device. Consumers already have them for personal use, but at the same time, they have become standard equipment in some offices.

Today's popular consumer devices do have "issues" on the job site. First, there is the screen's readability. The screen of a smartphone is small, forces many of us to wear reading glasses and can be difficult to read in direct sun light. But beyond the many styles of reading glasses that are available and our ability to move into the shade, we can zoom into images and magnify details by pinching the screen. Second, the virtual keyboard with its small keys can be a challenge. But this can be dealt with by using a stylus. The need to type each character may not be a problem for long, however. Voice recognition and voice-to-text keys on keyboards may soon become a more universal option, as they already are with

Android devices, making touching keys on the screen obsolete. Applications like Dragon Dictation (free from Nuance Communication) are available on the iPhone. They let users create text and copy and paste it into other applications. Next, there are the issues associated with security. Early versions of Apple's iOS did have security flaws, but do not now seem to be an issue in current versions of the operating system. However, the use of an employee's personal handheld device in the workplace is becoming more common which creates its own set of security issues. Most companies start with the very basic requirement that employees use the password feature available on mobile devices. Other companies have a policy that if an employee leaves the company, or the device is lost or stolen, the company has the right to erase the device remotely. Finally, there is the issue of durability on a job site. Various types of covers can provide a high degree of protection for smartphones and tablets. Covering a tablet with the OtterBox is like providing it with a turtle's shell. The "issues" many have with using these complex devices in the field are, in fact, manageable.

The tablet model is, ironically, older than the smartphone. It has made a comeback as the device of choice on the job site because of its larger touchscreen and its ability to handle the same applications that smartphones do. For many employees, however, the pocketsize smartphone form is attractive, convenient, and fun to use. But more screen real estate is the feature that is most important to construction industry professionals who deal with the fine line work of drawing images, so the tablet may win. The use of both devices at the same time seems to be the solution for the design and construction professional. Use the smartphone to communicate with the office while at the same time use the tablet to look at a drawing on the larger screen.

▶ A Match That Was Meant to Be ◀

Construction is a competitive business, and managing a construction project means keeping track of an ever-expanding collection of people, information, and materials. In addition, there are far more participants involved in the process than ever before, and much more regulatory oversight. More regulation means more documentation and more information. Managing a project just can't be done with paper documents any more. Project managers need all the modern technology they can get their hands on to keep everyone informed. So the convergence of the construction site and advanced technology is upon us.

Of all the technology that is available, none is more suited to the construction industry than the smartphone and tablet. Mobile technology is perfect for enhancing work-flow because construction is by definition a very mobile activity, with multiple tasks spread out over multiple sites, and with each project having a loosely associated group of stakeholders who change with each project. The files produced by powerful, office-based production platforms can now, in the proper format, be easily transmitted to and presented by, these highly mobile, field-based presentation platforms.

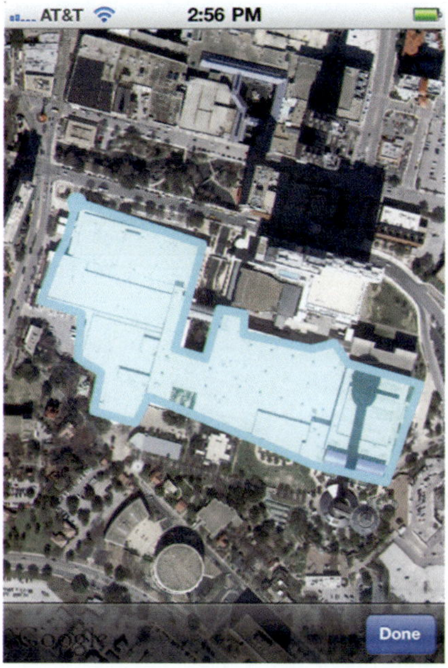

II.
Consolidation, Communication and Collaboration

For the first hundred years of consumer communications, there were relatively few changes. Not until the late 1970s did the first commercial cellular networks come into being, and some of us still remember the plain, black rotary telephones that we rented from the phone company. Today, a cell phone is not just a phone; it is a mobile, multifunction device. The tendency of carriers to make strategic and exclusive alliances with phone manufacturers brought us a whole new world of subsidized smartphones. This business model has been the single largest contributor to the popularization of the smartphone.

With respect to the relationship between today's job sites and websites, the question still is: How can we use these developments to do a better job of managing larger teams and keep everyone on the same page?

▶ Synchronization ◀

Not long ago most synchronization for a construction project ended when a reproduction company produced multiple sets of drawings and specifications, and delivered them to plan rooms and bidders. After that the process involved producing addenda and hammering out what was the design intent and what were "means and methods." It was an adversarial relationship. Today we have more negotiated contracts, teamwork, and better coordination. Drawings are now produced on modern CAD (computer aided design) platforms with state-of-the-art software. But plans, sections, elevations, and details are still plotted on paper at the office or by a reproduction company off-site and then delivered. The process can take days before the paper documents are finally distributed to all of the stakeholders. Paper is still the medium for communicating ideas, just as it has been for a long, long time. Recently we've seen online FTP (file transfer protocol) and FTH (file transaction hub) sites appear. PDF files are uploaded by the design firm and downloaded by the contractors and subcontractors. Teamwork has improved. But the directions in the field for getting a building built still wind up on paper, along with all of the associated distribution and revision challenges.

When a change is made to one of the sheets, the original drawing file has to be revised electronically, and the process is repeated. This in itself is not difficult, but the work is re-rendered on paper once again, many times with delays and additional expense. Each revision is just as cumbersome to produce as the original drawing. And then even once the reproductions are made, each stakeholder needs to receive the document, file it and many times personalize it with comments. The use of 8½ x 11 supplemental drawings, sketches, and lists associated with that drawing are then attached. All of those additions stay with each stakeholder and are usually hand-written. Drawings are stuck in endless informal silos. The result is different stakeholders with different visions of the project.

The goal is to keep all of the changing documents in the hands of a growing number of team members.

We long ago moved to the electronic production of documents with CAD software, and now it's time to take the next step and move to the electronic presentation, sharing, updating, and synchronization of that information. The old model of paper updates and paper distribution is obsolete. It's far more efficient to use mobile platforms in the field, and use easily sharable and editable electronic documents.

Some of the advantages of this approach are the following:

Eliminate the need to have each version of a document reproduced on paper either at the office or by a reproduction company

Ensure everyone on the project team has the same drawings, the same notes and the same version of the information

Share information and drawings quickly and easily with stakeholders, regardless of location

Improve the productivity and information flow of the construction process

Increasing the speed at which information is distributed, incidentally, does have one disadvantage. Producing complex structures requires thought and care. If information arrives so fast that we don't have time to consider its implications, the final product may wind up being "thoughtless." And if we are constantly bombarded with bits of information from different sources, how can we possibly keep track of it all? Contemporary file management systems and reasonable schedules that allow for quality workmanship are required.

For a technology to be truly significant, it must support our desire to produce more products of better quality, more economically. Just think of all of the time and material resources that could be saved if we eliminated the use of paper. We now produce documents in an electronic form in the office. There is no reason why we can't keep this form of information in the field.

Modern mobile technology in the construction industry is moving us toward better synchronization of an ever growing number of construction team members. The smartphone is first and foremost a communications device. Its emphasis is on voice, but it can also help us communicate through pictures and drawings. The tablet is a drawing presentation platform that is a logical extension of our office-based drawing production platforms. The synchronization of drawings between stakeholders in a project currently occurs via FTP and FTH sites and service providers like Google Docs. The drawings are uploaded by the producers and downloaded by the users. But we now are moving toward the use of services and applications like Dropbox (free from Dropbox, Inc.)

that automatically sync the contents of directories on office production platforms to the same directories on mobile platforms. Apple's new iCloud service will expand and refine this concept yet again. End users are thus able to receive drawing images as well as sketched changes to an image with notes, and then have those edits immediately pushed out to all stakeholders in all locations. Everyone has access to the latest information, the latest iteration of each drawing, and the latest notes and suggestions made by the construction team on the job site.

We have moved from the distribution of information via CDs and email to online FTP and FTH sites to services that make documents appear on our mobile devices out of thin air. Today's synchronization challenges need the best document organization solutions possible. Different email accounts that are specifically named to send, receive and hold different types of information are the solution.

▶ Construction in the "Cloud" ◀

Cloud computing has had an impact on just about everything, but it is often misunderstood. The name alone confuses people. "Cloud" sounds like something that is hard to pin down, but in reality, it's very simple. Cloud computing is the storage of information or the providing of functionality at third-party servers which is delivered over the internet as a service. When you use Gmail or Hotmail, for example, the actual email client isn't in your computer on your desktop. It's on one of Google's or Microsoft's servers. You access your email over the internet, but the actual email-client software and the emails themselves are somewhere else. That's the cloud.

Cloud computing and SaaS have gained popularity in many consumer areas. Besides Hotmail and other free email platforms, consumers love to use sites like Flickr to store photographs. The online services and systems that are now in place to share pictures of the kids could just as easily be used to share images of drawings. Google has a complete set of SaaS applications that help you be more productive, without having the software or the files reside on your computer.

Cloud computing makes the use of mobile platforms even more attractive. When you are using a cloud application, you can access that application (and your data) from any computer or handheld device with a browser, at any location. Whether you're at the office, at home, or at the job site, and whether you're using your work computer, your home laptop, or your smartphone, you can still get to the same information and do the same things, all without the need for massive hard disks.

Cloud computing provides more than just consumer convenience. The technology is robust, and the model is solid enough so that it has been embraced by small and large businesses all over the world.

The cloud is the ultimate mobile tool because it supports easy access to, and sharing of, information. Businesses have been taking on a much more global perspective ever since the dawn of the internet age, and today the infrastructure is in place for even a small company to have clients and partners in other countries. Cloud computing is a natural extension of this trend. If you're an American contractor, and you're bidding on a job in Saudi Arabia, you need to have an easy way to communicate and share data. Shipping paper documents back and forth between the home office and a job site on the other side of the world is just not practical. The combination of cloud computing and mobile technology is bringing the construction industry into the twenty first century, and it will be increasingly difficult for companies to compete and survive without it.

▶ Teams Are Getting Bigger ◀

One of the most important reasons why project teams are getting bigger is because of specialization.

Of course, the construction industry has always relied on consultants and subcontractors, but today with the increase in the complexity of materials, systems and regulations, we now have endless specialists for waterproofing, acoustics, interior design, ADA, and more. Specialization has even created the "design" firm category as opposed to the "general practice" firm. Many times, these different team members are in different geographic locations across town, across the country, or on the other side of the world.

There is another reason for the increasing number of specialists. It is called "liability shedding." Architects and designers often don't want to assume liability for various aspects of a building, so they bring in consultants who are knowledgeable in those specific areas, for example waterproofing. This helps to shield the architect from liability should something go wrong, while at the same time ensuring that certain critical aspects of the project are thought through by the most qualified person. The result is that the construction team expands.

But the increasing number of specialists and consultants involved in a project isn't just the result of a fear of litigation. It's also the result of the increasing complexity of materials, systems and designs. Architects and contractors are by nature generalists. They coordinate and manage the overall project and rely on subcontractors and specialists to manage individual aspects of the project.

With every construction project involving multiple team members, many of whom are independent professionals not employed directly by the design or construction firm, project management becomes especially critical, especially under difficult time constraints. The project manager must make sure that everyone involved is in synch and informed. He must not allow the size of the team to bog down the process.

▶ How Project Documentation Might Evolve ◀

Not long ago we produced drawings based on the client's direction and then built the project. Design, Bid, Build projects seem so quaint these days. Now we produce documentation for different parts of the project, permit them and issue them to the field at different times. We "fast track" more and more projects. Each aspect of the work requires multiple specialists, often in different parts of the country or overseas. Project complexity is expanding, while project schedules are collapsing. As a result, construction requires increased sophistication with respect to management and coordination. This requires rethinking the way we communicate and coordinate our documents.

What might a contemporary work-flow be if we took full advantage of the systems that are now available to us? First, drawings and specifications could be issued, with proper degrees of security via cloud-based systems like Dropbox or iCloud. Those requiring that documents be printed could still download and print them. But those preferring to use mobile devices could have access to the document files and call them up on the screens of their smartphones or tablets at any time. The document directory could also be kept current, with revisions by the issuing firm simply by loading new files into the cloud-based directory. Documents, if issued in a JPG format, could appear as thumbnails on mobile devices and searched easily for content. If the documents were issued as PDF files, images could be called to the screen of mobile devices, and screen captures could be produced as needed. These images could then be marked up using any of the many mobile applications that are now on the market. Specifications could also be issued as PDF files and loaded into the cloud-based directory. Documents can now be pushed directly from the systems of the issuing team member to the screens of the smartphones and tablets of team members in the field.

iPad Photo Albums

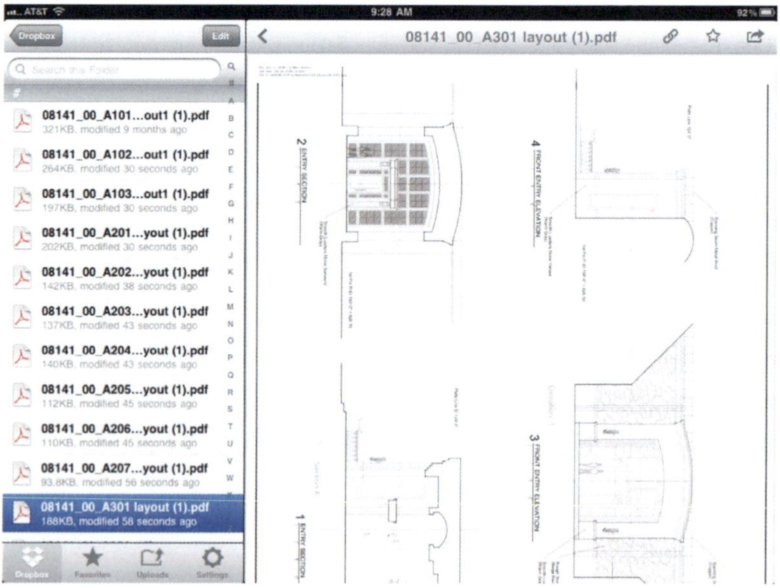

Dropbox on iPad

III.
The Internet and Spheres of Influence

A business is no longer defined by physical boundaries. This is the result of several factors that include globalization, advanced communications technology, the internet, and an increasing acceptance of telecommuting, teleworking, and outsourcing. Some of these factors may be debatable, and there are those who decry globalization and outsourcing, but the fact is, it is here to stay. The era of the purely local business is over, and for better or worse, it's not coming back. What we have to do now is embrace the technology and the new business model, and figure out how to turn it to our advantage.

▶ Thinking Globally ◀

A business of any size, even before these changes took place, always relied on its sphere of influence. That sphere of influence included the people whom the business would interact with, such as customers, the owner's friends at trade associations or the local chamber of commerce. These venues have always been a strong source of business development. Today, that sphere of influence has greatly expanded because of the internet and social networking.

In the construction industry, a business's sphere of influence is vital to a company's success. Construction has always been a referral type of business, and success depends on a business' connections as well as the quality of its work.

This is very relevant to the modern design and construction company that is attempting to embrace technology to stay competitive. We've been discussing how smartphones are revolutionizing the business of producing projects, but they can also be used to advertise and gain a competitive advantage. Specifically, current handheld device technology can be used to project the business' positive attitude toward change.

Our sphere of influence and how we manage it make a difference, especially once we move to mobile platforms like the smartphone and tablet. These devices let us work more closely with each other, and they make it possible for us to bring in more stakeholders from other fields of expertise.

It is important that we change our attitudes. Our network is no longer local. Our network may just as easily come from people we have connected with on LinkedIn or Facebook, or who live in another city but possess specialized skills that are vital to our projects. We can use these social networking tools to expand our sphere of influence. We can cast a wider net in looking for the best experts and specialists. Or, if you are a specialist who caters to the design and construction industry, you are no longer tied to serving professionals in your local community. Anyone can now just as easily offer consulting services to clients in Bangkok as they do to clients in Biloxi.

▶ Finding Your Global Team ◀

English is still the language of choice when it comes to communicating with the world, and it is possible to have an extended English-speaking team that spans the globe. Our office may be in Chicago, but we can have a programmer in India, a copywriter in San Francisco, and a graphic designer in London, and all of them can be paid via PayPal. It is now possible for an individual or a small company to be a global company.

One way to expand our team is through B2B (business to business) sites like Elance.com, which lets us create a virtual team without regard to geographic location. These sites let us take full advantage of the outsourcing model, simply by placing a detailed description of our project on the site, issuing an RFP (request for proposal), taking and reviewing bids, and then working with our new contractor to get the work done.

Here are a few basic rules for being successful with sites like Elance:

1. Be clear about the scope of the work and the budget.
2. Don't let price obscure quality. Like any marketplace, there are those on Elance who have more skills and those who have less. No experience or educational requirements are required to register as a provider. So be careful to look over the provider's history and profile, and be prepared to pay more money

for better qualifications. Don't just take the lowest bid.

3. Remember that foreign service providers can be just as skilled as domestic ones. India for example, has some of the world's finest technical institutions, and you can find excellent programmers there.
4. Be prepared for a language barrier even if all of the parties communicate in English. A project can easily break down due to poor communications. Some of the larger Indian outsourcing firms have English-speaking, U.S. based liaisons with whom you can deal directly.
5. Keep the lines of communication open. Some of the less professional providers on Elance and other boards want to work anonymously. That's a big mistake for them and a disaster for you. Don't choose a provider who refuses to talk to you on the phone. A true professional will always make himself or herself available. Use Skype and deal with them face to face.
6. Use the Elance communications and payment tools with contractors rather than direct email, so that if a dispute occurs, the Elance arbitration system has access to the documentation associated with the issue.

It is also possible to secure work through "global competitions," like those managed by 99designs.com. The service consumer posts a design brief or concept description that details the work that needs to be done, and service providers compete by posting their work to the consumer's account. A cash award is offered as the prize for the winning concept. Larger prizes mean more participation and a higher level of work quality. Service providers from all over the world can post work, and the service consumer can eliminate entries at any time.

I've had experience with both services and contractors in foreign countries. The results have been mixed. It can be very exciting to work with an individual or company on the other side of the world. But the difficulties associated with language and the quality of work, with respect to applications development, suggests limiting collaboration to prototyping rather than the development of finished products. This venue is the most economical approach to the testing of ideas and the development of preliminary concepts. On the other hand, this is a way to develop relationships with individuals and companies around the world that can have a different and valuable perspective on the issues.

▶ Concept Communication with Pictures ◀

Design and construction professionals are in the concept communications business, and our preferred form of communication is with drawings and pictures. Drawings and pictures, like music, are a universal language and have been used for centuries to convey ideas. A picture taken by a smartphone is still worth a thousand words. It can be very useful when dealing with contractors in other countries where there may be a language barrier.

Smartphone cameras can produce high-quality photographs. They can also produce pictures of any image that can be brought to the screen of the device. The iPhone's ability to produce a screen capture may not have received the kind of attention it should have as a technique for communicating concepts. Screen captures can be taken of websites that display product literature, aerial views of sites produced by mapping applications or details of text or graphics in PDF files. After producing the screen capture, the image is saved to the same photo album that contains the photographs taken by the camera. Both the photos and the screen captures can then be sent via email with just a few taps on the screen. These images can also be brought into applications that are designed to edit photos, like Adobe Photoshop Express (free from Adobe Systems, Inc.). This application can rotate and crop an image, and it includes a number of features for enhancing the quality of the image.

Marking up or "red lining" drawings or pictures is a technique that design and construction professionals are very familiar with. Today, however, marking up images, including those of drawings, has become a digital process that happens on mobile devices. Drawings as we have known them have changed from lines on paper to pixels or vectors within an electronic file that can be sent across the world in seconds. Global networks now move mobile documents.

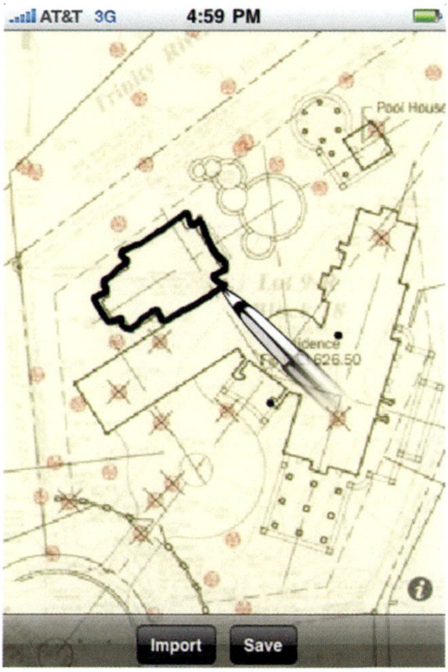

IV.
Mobile Drawings and Specifications

Today, trade and commerce are global. The barriers of distance and location no longer limit individuals and organizations. No business enterprise, no matter its size, needs to confine itself to local boundaries; the world is open to exploration. This remarkable transformation has happened because of the internet and the growth in communications technology. Globalization and outsourcing have further reduced the size of the world, and teleworking and telecommuting are commonplace business operations.

To facilitate this new way of doing business, the design and construction industry must embrace a new and more mobile method of communicating and sharing information. This means rethinking the way we communicate through drawings and specifications, which in the past have been bulky and difficult to share. Getting drawings and documents onto mobile platforms is the logical next step in this transition.

▶ Impact on the Construction Industry ◀

The word "drawings" no longer seems appropriate. Today's technologies are having an impact on almost every aspect of life across the globe, and so it is with the way construction professionals communicate. Whether on a personal or professional level, the internet and other technologies have swept across the world, changing lives and the way people live and work. In the design and construction industry, technology has produced several new tools that have changed the way architects, engineers, contractors, and interior designers produce and exchange drawings. We produce drawing files that can be transmitted via email across the world instantly. It seems entirely logical that the multi-megabyte electronic files that are created by powerful office-based production platforms be moved, in a more compact file format, to our new highly mobile presentation platforms that we carry into the field. Now with the tablet and the various models of the smartphones, including the iPhone, mobile applications can be used to manage and edit "mobile drawings". We can call up a mobile drawing anytime, anywhere. We can sketch an idea, place a note on it, and email the image to team members with a few taps on the screen.

▶ Mobile Drawings Management ◀

Managing multi-megabyte drawing files quickly is beyond the power of handheld devices as these devices exist today. They are not yet fully functional computers that have the power of desktops and laptops. However, the product of our CAD and BIM (building information modeling) systems can still be displayed on our mobile devices if they are issued in a compact, less editable PDF or JPG form. Plans, sections, elevations, details and schedules are the way construction professionals communicate their instructions to the field and these file formats limit the ability of others to edit them which is still an important objective with many organizations.

The standard file format today for issuing instructions is the Adobe PDF file. This file type has a number of advantages. PDF files are dimensionally stable when printed, clear and sharp on the screens of handheld devices, and reasonable in file size. Programs like Adobe Reader and applications like GoodReader for iPhone (Yuri Selukoff, $4.99), which can markup PDF files are extremely useful. An alternative to this file format is JPG or BMP. These file types can also have reasonable file sizes. There are problems, however, with the resolution if the magnification of the image is too great. On the other hand, they are consistent with the image management systems that already exist on handheld devices for photographs. This lets a design and construction professional keep his mobile drawings for a particular project together in an album or directory with all of the photographs and screen captures associated with a project. This format is also consistent with all of the online image management sites on the internet like Flickr or Picasa. These images can also be enhanced by using applications designed to touch-up photos.

But one of the most important advantages of using the JPG or BMP format for mobile drawings is thumbnails. Seeing even a small rendering of the contents of a file is extremely helpful when searching through possibly hundreds of mobile drawings for a project. The idea of the thumbnail has always been associated with photographs, and if our mobile drawings are the same file type, this convenience can be associated with our drawings as well. At this time there isn't a convenient way to generate thumbnails of PDF files for handheld devices.

For mobile construction drawings to be truly useful, they must perform as well as lines on paper and display the fine line work and variations in line weight that make drawings read well. Using both formats may be a way to make the most of each file type's advantages. PDF files are the standard of the trade and can be transmitted and read on the screen of handheld devices. The user can bring one of these images to the screen, zoom into the part of the image of interest, and perform a screen capture. This image can then be marked up or enhanced by any of the mobile applications designed to edit JPG images.

But how do we move the PDF or JPG mobile drawings produced by our office production platforms to our mobile presentation platforms? The easiest and most straightforward way is to create an email, attach the image, and transmit it to an email account on the mobile device. Most smartphones and tablets allow the saving of images that are attached to emails to a specific location on the device. Another way to transfer mobile drawings from the desktop computer to the mobile device is by syncing. On the iPhone, this is done through iTunes. This software transfers any music, video, and so on purchased through iTunes to the iPhone or iPad. It also transfers photos and mobile drawings in the directory structure you set up for your desktop to the same directory structure on your iPhone. Albums that were originally designed for pictures of the kids or the vacation can just as easily have job numbers for projects. Online services also let users organize and load directories on their desktops with photos or mobile drawings and have them synced automatically via the cloud. One of the most popular applications for using this technique, as mentioned earlier, is Dropbox. When you move files into your Dropbox directory on your desktop, they immediately appear in all of the same Dropbox application directories that are present on your mobile devices.

Recently, Apple announced a major upgrade to its cloud based document sharing service. iCloud is going to be a major upgrade to its MobileMe and iDisk services, and will accelerate the use of cloud-based music, applications and books. iCloud is also going to be an effortless way to sync photos and mobile drawings on desktop, laptop and handheld devices and will compete with the already popular Google and Android services.

Software and applications for transferring mobile drawings between devices are available for little or no cost. More sophisticated file management and file sharing systems are available to design and construction professionals. But the inexpensive, easy-to-use and readily available tools that are already present on today's mobile devices can be made to work just as effectively and much more economically. Once mobile drawings become available on mobile devices, the tasks traditionally associated with paper drawings will become electronic. Applications specific to the way design and construction professionals work with mobile drawings are available and they will be discussed in Chapter VII.

▶ Document Presentation and Management ◀

Drawings in the construction industry indicate quantity and location, while specifications communicate quality. Just as we can present our drawings in a mobile format, so too can we present our specifications in a mobile format. The advent of eBooks has made the possibility of having a mobile copy of the specifications for a project on our smartphones or tablets a reality. Design and construction professionals can self-publish their specifications and make copies available to the construction team. This is already being done to some extent with PDF file versions of documents, but the features associated with eBooks could significantly change the way specifications are written.

Two features associated with the iPad and iPhone are particularly useful for mobile drawings and specifications management. These are high-resolution screens and "gestures" or the ability to issue commands with different combinations of fingers touching the screen. The iPad has a screen that shows images clearly, and a user can zoom in and out of them easily. Users can also download eBooks and go through the pages simply by flipping through them with a finger. If books can be flipped through and read, why not project manuals? A company could even issue its specifications via iBooks with links to drawings and product websites and have the entire set of documents needed for a particular project in one file on a handheld device. Everything can then be taken with us to a meeting, to a showroom, or to the job site. This even opens up the possibility of preloading a tablet with a complete set of mobile drawings and specifications, shipping the device to a remote site on the other side of the world, and keeping it current via the cloud.

The Changing Scenario

Underwriter's Laboratories now has an ad for a mobile version of its fire-rated construction details. The application is called UL Connect (free from Underwriter's Laboratories Inc.) and contains certification information and code compliance tools. Soon the IBC, IPC, IMC, NEC,IFC, IECC and so on will probably have apps that let you look up code sections. Handheld devices, in particular the iPhone, have become so popular that companies like UL now see that they can take advantage of the mobility and convenience of these devices to make information more accessible to customers.

New models of handheld devices and operating system enhancements are being introduced in the marketplace constantly. This variety is giving design and construction professionals more and more options for customizing their devices, so that they support, rather than limit, their personal working styles. The construction industry can take full advantage of these emerging technologies to enhance productivity. Design and construction professionals who elect to move forward and combine their field experience with these powerful modern tools will improve the productivity of their companies and the industry.

When we are able to do more with less, we save time, money, and resources. Being environmentally conscious is no longer the stuff of environmentalists. It's just good business. Businesses that acknowledge this can improve their position in the marketplace. The idea of creating electronic documents, drawings, and specifications for sharing and distribution on mobile platforms is a big win for the environment. Just think of all of the paper, transportation, and disposal costs that are saved when we switch to the use of mobile drawings and specifications. This approach is one way companies can establish their environmental bona fides and advertise themselves as green, responsible organizations.

▶ Return on Investment ◀

Are smartphones and tablets tools or toys? The similarities between the current market for smartphones and the market for the first PCs are interesting. In both cases, the devices are and were more popular with young people. The first Apple computers started out in schools, and so too has the iPhone. The software and applications for both PC's and smartphones were and are heavily weighted toward playing games and having fun. It wasn't until late in the development of the PC that businesses started to integrate them into the way they worked. This happened only after business-oriented software for spread-sheets and word processing arrived. More and more, business and productivity applications are appearing today for smartphones.

Unlike the early days of the PC, however, the initial investment in the hardware and software for smartphones is minimal. The devices and the applications that run on them have intuitive interfaces, and many of the most productive applications are free. Data plans and contracts with carriers are required, but these agreements are straight forward.

When compared to the investment required for BIM hardware and software, the training for operators to be productive, and the complex technical issues that must be managed, smartphones and tablets are very attractive investments that can show returns in productivity quickly. Placing easy-to-use systems in the hands of more individuals means more people being more productive. Why not distribute easy-to-use devices and applications to a broad segment of the workforce rather than concentrate complex BIM systems in the hands of a few individuals? All of the students who are now in school will one day be employees, and they will bring their skills with mobile devices with them. Why not position our companies to take advantage of these skills?

When we integrate handheld devices and their applications into the way we do business, we will see opportunities for the production of new products and services. Easy-to-use tools do not have complex procedures that inhibit creative and experienced individuals from devising new ways to use them. They give individuals more freedom to respond to unforeseen circumstances in their own way. They support and encourage individual initiatives. The gatekeepers in IT departments who are usually the only ones familiar with the complex systems that the rest of us have to use, may lose some of their status as we become more mobile. On the other hand, IT departments could be repurposed and become an important part of our new mobile computing initiatives.

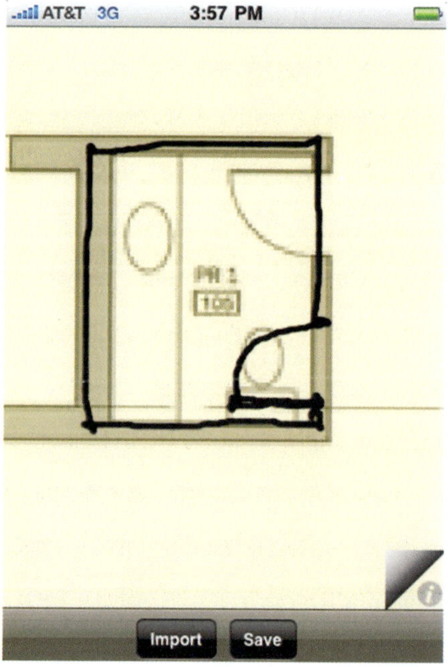

V.
Diversifying the Company

Diversification has always been critical to an organization's success. Companies must have a broad product line for customers, and design and construction firms are no different. McDonald's and Burger King have their flagship products but have responded to trends in the marketplace by introducing new items for their menus. They have diversified into gourmet coffee drinks and introduced salads that cater to the desire for healthier lifestyles. Google made its name by developing the world's greatest search engine, but now the company is much more than that. It has diversified into telecommunications and handheld devices with the introduction of Android smartphones. Warren Buffet is a master of diversification, too. The conglomerate he has assembled in Berkshire Hathaway has produced an astoundingly consistent and profitable performance for decades.

These companies and individuals watch changes in the marketplace, anticipate events, and produce new products and services that are properly positioned to respond to changes. They take reasonable risks. Design and construction professionals are in the business of producing visions that help clients assess the risks associated with construction projects. We create visions for others on a regular basis and now need to visualize a new future for ourselves. We need to become more entrepreneurial and create new products and services for new markets.

▶ New Products and Services ◀

Many design and construction professionals, faced with a lengthy recession and a slow and questionable economic recovery, must diversify or go out of business. Architects and interior designers for example, have a variety of skills that could help them diversify. Developing handheld device applications that satisfy client objectives is one of them. Engineers and contractors are also very close to the production of projects and can see what the challenges are for those in the field. These professionals have the esthetic, technical, management, and marketing skills to produce applications for smartphones and tablets.

The specifics associated with producing applications will be discussed in Chapter VI. But what resources do construction professionals have that can help them make such a transformation? First, construction professionals have an established client base. Many companies tend to specialize in a project type and become very familiar with the issues that affect their clients. Older firms could use their broader project knowledge base as an advantage over younger, more technically proficient competitors as a source for new product ideas.

Next, construction professionals have vast libraries of archived projects. This resource can be utilized to renew old relationships in a new way if the firm, for example, were to load an iPad with the floor plans for a past project and present it to a client's building maintenance department. A convenient way to carry and access technical documents for projects could significantly impact the efficiency of property management companies as well.

Finally, construction professionals have established graphics and IT capabilities that could be utilized in a new way. Individuals or departments with graphics abilities are well aware of the need for clear and concise applications interfaces. Established IT departments have very capable technical personnel who could probably do much more than maintain existing office systems. These departments and individuals could easily become billable entities, rather than overhead, if they were to train clients in the use of these new devices or produce the code for new applications.

The numbers and types of documents that owners deal with can be staggering. Construction professionals can offer owners ideas for mobile systems and applications that can help them maintain their facilities more effectively. Construction professionals can also look to another source for application ideas: employees. The individuals who produce the projects see the issues and solutions associated with their work. Many of them, fresh from school, already have amazing skills with mobile devices and know what works and what does not.

▶ The Global Marketplace ◀

Selling applications through Apple's App Store or the Android Market can give design and construction companies a global presence. The problems that are identified and solutions that are developed for clients in this country more than likely will be equally valuable to building owners, maintenance departments and property developers in other countries. The distribution of applications designed to address an industry issue is also a way to attract new clients that could use the firm's expertise.

Applications advertising is how companies that provide custom solutions to specific problems can expand their sphere of influence. Within an application there are a number of ways to put the firm's credentials before potential clients. One of the easiest is the page curl feature. At the bottom corners of the handheld device screen, a graphic can be added that, when touched, flips up the image to reveal a standalone screen that can contain information about the firm, a link to the firm's website or a link to a promotional video. Advertising space within applications via iAds is also popular. Applications can solve problems for users and be a vehicle for presenting the name of the developer to a new and broader client base at the same time.

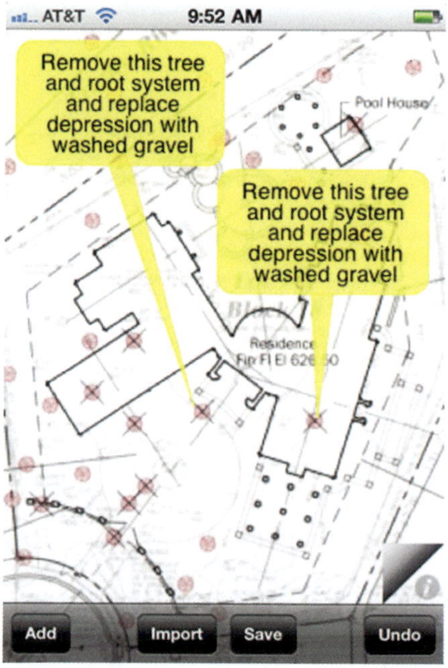

VI.
Producing an Application

Although the list is growing, there are still very few companies producing smartphones and tablets. Major barriers to entry include the need for enormous amounts of money, technical ability, and vision. Development of relationships with retailers and carriers is also a considerable undertaking. As a result, smartphone and tablet hardware will likely continue to be dominated by a relatively small handful of large companies.

On the other hand, tens of thousands of developers are creating the applications that run on these devices. The barriers to entry for becoming a smartphone application developer are very small. For just a few thousand dollars, anyone can purchase the appropriate SDK (software development kit), produce an entertaining or useful application, and sell it. In fact, new development and simulation platforms have made it remarkably easy to create applications. A special symbiotic relationship has developed between manufacturers and developers. The field of applications development is wide open to the design and construction industry. As time goes by, the interest in design, construction, engineering and property development applications will grow.

▶ The Essence of Applications Development ◀

Design and construction professionals are very familiar with the business of producing a concept, documenting that concept so that others can understand it, building support for the concept with various stakeholders, securing approvals, and producing the project. They are managers who understand the big picture as well as the implications of the details. Design and construction professionals have the project management skills that are required to produce applications for smartphones and tablets.

In the development of smartphone applications, it is important to distinguish between the responsibilities of the project manager, the code writer and the graphic artist. Sitting down and producing the code for an application is an important part of its creation, but the way the application looks and feels is crucial. Creating an application is a project management exercise. Just like a construction project, we use consultants, subcontractors, and third-party suppliers who are skilled in their particular fields. Design and construction professionals are well qualified to manage this process and mediate between the demands of the design, its functionality, and the time and cost implications.

The application development process varies, but generally it starts with thoroughly vetting the idea and making sure there is a strong business case for it. What will the app do? Who is the app for? Does the app need to be profitable or is there another goal? Will the app connect to a database or have a website? What is the name of the application? Next, the application's functionality must be defined. Sketched storyboards show how the application flows from screen to screen. Cutting and pasting images, with modifications, from other applications that are similar in look and feel is a popular technique. All of this work should be organized within a design concept document that can be used to develop a consensus and to secure proposals for graphics and code development work. A balance between simplicity and variety must be reached within this document. Next, more finished screens, not necessarily artistically correct, need to be developed. Finally, the code for the application's functionality and the linking of the final screens occurs, along with extensive testing of the product. This process is very familiar to the design and construction professional. It covers schematic design, design development, construction documents, construction, and project closeout.

With respect to the development of applications that are specific to the construction industry, who is better positioned to understand the issues that facilities owners and managers face than architects, engineers, contractors, and interior designers? Why not apply this "local knowledge" and professionalism to the task of producing applications that solve real problems for these clients?

▶ Lessons Learned ◀

The following are some of my observations concerning the production of iPhone applications for the construction industry:

1. Almost as important as the application's concept, is the application's name and icon. The name of the application must communicate in less than eleven characters (the maximum number of characters that will fit under the application icon on the screen of an iPhone) what the application does. The icon must communicate in a graphic way, the same thing. The naming of applications is a challenge because so many of the most economical words are already taken for website names. Performing a search on Godaddy.com or Register.com to see what words are not already being used is the first step. The applications icon needs to be well designed by a graphic artist because it communicates in a subliminal way the functionality, look, feel and quality of the app.
2. Anyone can define a problem that can be addressed by a mobile application. Property owners, managers, and agents can provide this input but so too can employees of your own company. These are the people who are constantly presented with challenges that need solutions. Simple techniques that have been developed over years of trial and

error are excellent candidates for application concepts.

3. The production of a dynamic concept document is very familiar to design professionals. A thoroughly vetted, written and illustrated description of the problem, and the way the application will deal with it, is the most important part of the project. It is the starting point of the development effort. The document can be used to communicate work-flow, secure proposals from programmers and graphic artists, and build a consensus with stakeholders. As is the case with design development drawings for construction projects, revisions to this document are much easier to make after receiving feedback than once the project is underway.
4. The orientation of the application on the screen of the device can be portrait, landscape, or both. If the application is to run in both portrait and landscape modes, multiple variations of the graphics for the interface have to be produced. This can lead to confusion and a loss of production time if it is not addressed in the concept document.

5. On Apple devices, applications can be formatted for the iPhone, iPad or both. Applications formatted only for the iPhone will run on the iPad but with a loss of resolution.
6. The number of smartphone and tablet hardware platforms is large and growing, but the number of operating systems for the applications that run on them remains reasonable. The major players in operating systems are Apple's iOS, Android, and Windows Mobile. The code for one operating system does not transfer to another, but if the functionality for one device and its operating system is worked out and clear, then developing for other platforms is easier.
7. During the production of the code for an application, the programmer submits a series of builds or versions that run only on the device of the person responsible for testing and feedback. The individual responsible for testing then emails feedback back to the programmer. This can be a long and drawn-out process, depending on the complexity of the application and the ability of the two parties to communicate.
8. Focus groups or feedback from others in the industry can be very helpful during the

testing of builds for an application. Inevitably, compromises need to be made, and the opinions of others, possibly users, can be very valuable. Feedback during this time can also provide the beginning of a list of features for future versions of the application after it is issued.

9. Prior to submitting an application for sale and distribution by Apple, application owners must establish an account. The names of the individuals in charge of the various aspects of the application's development are required, as is bank account information for the direct deposit of sales revenue. A nominal fee is associated with the establishing of this account, and it must be renewed annually.
10. After the application has been thoroughly tested, it is submitted to Apple for review and approval. The name of the application, the graphics associated with the icon, the price of the app, and the code must be submitted to an online location set aside by Apple. The approval process can take from two to six weeks but can sometimes occur sooner. Apple takes 30 percent of the sales for its distribution of applications. Apple is very careful about the content and functionality

of applications. The Android Market, on the other hand, is more open.

11. Pricing of applications is very subjective. A price that is too high can eliminate buyers, while pricing too low makes the app seem cheap and makes the chances for recouping production costs that much more difficult. Many applications are free. Many times they have limited capability with an offer by the developer to provide a full-featured application at an additional cost. Sometimes applications are free because they are being used as marketing tools. Applications, their names, and their functionality are intellectual property that will one day have value in ways that we cannot yet see.
12. Getting the word out regarding an application, and trying to separate it from the hundreds of thousands of apps in Apple's App Store, is a challenge. The type of application greatly affects how the app needs to be presented. Promotion by reviewers or bloggers is one way, and print advertising is another. Facebook and Twitter sites can be useful. Even books, like this one, that present an application within a larger context are an option.

13. The how-to video has also become an important part of marketing initiatives for many industries, especially with the popularity of YouTube and the availability of convenient video production tools. Marketing studies have shown that videos are very effective at getting a message across and generate a much higher conversion rate than any other type of marketing message. Creating a how-to video is easy with handheld devices. To make it effective, however, the video needs to be professionally produced. The expense associated with engaging a professional scriptwriter and video production team can be money well spent. AppShows.com is a firm that specializes in this type of work.
14. A website with the name of the application is relatively easy to set up. These websites can contain different kinds of information regarding the application, from how-to videos to FAQs to blogs. A link to the application's supporting website can also be a part of the application interface and is sometimes located on the page-curl screen of the app.
15. Presentations or speaking engagements are a good way to present the application, what it can do and why it exists. Presentations can

also be made via the internet using various services. Slideshare.com lets individuals and companies post presentations so that others can see something of the content and perhaps be motivated to ask for a live presentation.

16. Apple's App Store gives users an opportunity to leave feedback regarding an application and rate it. User feedback is extremely valuable, even when it is negative. There's really no way to respond to negative feedback, which can sometimes be based on simple misunderstandings, other than possibly through an application's supporting website blog. Developers do need to be prepared to give users their money back if they are dissatisfied.
17. Revisions to the application must be issued periodically. We can anticipate to some degree what the market wants, but only users can make the final determination. The best approach is to keep the concept for the application simple, do one thing well, and let the marketplace participate in the design through its feedback. Encourage feedback, take surveys, and start a blog or a forum for user communications.

18. Applications can sometimes be thought of as templates. If the functionality is there to address a certain need, perhaps the same functionality could also be applied toward addressing a need in another field. An application developed to catalog food recipes, for example, could, after changes to the application's graphics, be used to catalog office furniture or machine parts.

The concept of continuous improvement means that we are never really finished with an application. Every software development company takes this process to heart, out of necessity. Once a product has been released, customers will talk about it, bloggers will write about it, and users may complain about it. Updates do not necessarily indicate mistakes have been made. They are, however, an indication that the product is dynamic and flexible and can respond to the changing conditions of the industry and the marketplace.

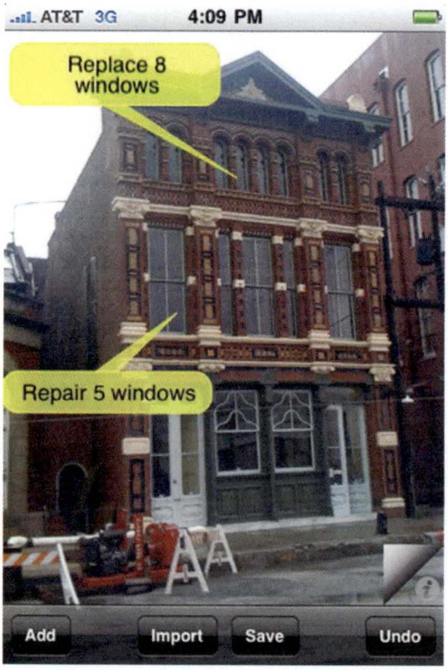

VII.
The Citygraphs Applications

Citygraphs was established in 2003. The goals for the company have evolved as the technology for handheld devices has changed, but a simple idea has always remained: Use the mobility of handheld devices to address issues where they occur. Citygraphs.com now produces mobile applications for design and construction professionals that communicate concepts with drawings and pictures. I have produced a series of applications that I would have liked when

I was walking projects and that I believe other design and construction professionals will find useful. I was always in a hurry on projects, so these applications are easy to use and perform a simple task. They are designed to run on Apple's iPhone and iPad and can be used to edit any electronic image that can be stored on the iPhone, whether they are photographs taken with the camera, mobile drawings synced to the iPhone's albums, or screen captures of other types of content. I believe these applications can save design and construction professionals' time and money and make the most of the mobility that smartphones and tablets now provide.

Below you will find not only a description the applications and how they operate, but an example of how they might be used on a project. Projects can move forward quickly and economically when stakeholders are present and engaged with the issue. Many times this happens away from the office at remote locations. Opportunities to engage all of those with a stake in the solution can't be allowed to slip away, especially when a project has a demanding time schedule. Handheld tools that we can carry in our pockets or under our arms, loaded with the information we need, make a team's decision making and documentation possible wherever we are.

▶ uScaleit+ ◀

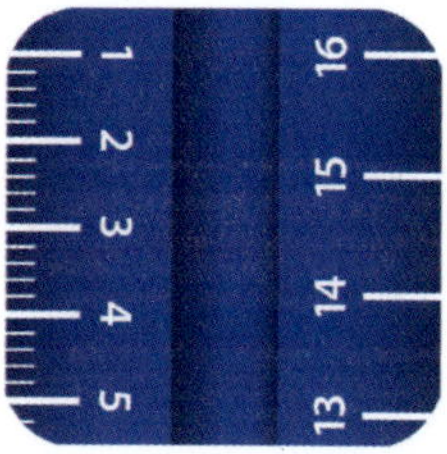

I recall being on a project site that had a beautiful shoreline by a lake. The owner asked me how many linear feet of retaining wall we would have to build along the shoreline to keep the ground from eroding. Of course, the calculation had to be done back at the office, where we had access to the drawings. But if I had had uScaleit+ at the time, I could have called up an aerial photograph of the site, created a linear measurement of the shoreline, and provided him with a figure within a few minutes.

uScaleit+ produces area and linear measurement estimates for any location in the world, using Google Maps. A user types in a landmark, address or zip code and is presented with an aerial photograph of that location. The user then zooms and pans the image to a specific location and touches "Done" to lock the image in place. Touching points on the screen produces calculations. A stylus can be used for a more accurate placement of points. Shaking the device clears the screen so that another calculation can be made. The application has a switch that can be used to present calculations in English or metric units and it is available when the user touches the page curl icon. Area calculations are presented in square feet, square yards, acres, and square miles or in square meters and square kilometers. Distance calculations can be presented in feet, yards and miles, or meters and kilometers. This application let's roofers, paving contractors, real estate agents, civil engineers, and land planners create area and linear measurement estimates while they are onsite. Estimates for rooftops, parking areas, bodies of water, property frontage, or shorelines can be generated. The application can produce calculations associated with disaster areas that use views of structures before the damage has occurred. The screen shots at the beginning of Chapters I, II, and III are examples of the work the application produces.

Feedback regarding the uScaleit+ application has centered on the desire for more precision in the placement of points on the screen. The application is for estimating purposes only, precisely because of the difficulty associated with placing points accurately with the tip of the finger. An estimating tool like uScaleit+, however, is many times all that is required by construction contractors for measurements of large pieces of property. Citygraphs does have plans to upgrade the application so that users can zoom into points after they have been placed and adjust their location prior to performing a calculation.

▶ uSketchit+ ◀

I was once called to a project that had a classroom ready for ceiling work. It was necessary to revise the locations of sprinkler heads on the ceiling plan because of unusual ceiling profiles and coverage requirements. The problem was solved, but it required a lot of back-and-forth with the sprinkler contractor after I returned to the office. If I had had uSketchit+ however, I could have called up the ceiling plan on my mobile device, located the sprinkler heads while I was there on the job site with the contractor, and emailed the plan with the new head locations to everyonc while standing there.

Numerous sketching applications for handheld devices let users create line work by dragging a finger across the screen. These sketching apps are fun but do not let you see where your line work is being placed when the point you touch on the screen is under your finger. You can use a stylus to get around this problem but when you're in the field without a stylus, and you need to mark up a drawing or a photograph of a job condition, what do you do? uSketchit+ is an application that addresses this problem and simulates a process that design professionals are very familiar with. It simulates the use of a fat black pen on yellow tracing paper that has been placed over a drawing. When your finger touches the screen, it activates a virtual pen with a tip that appears just beyond your finger tip, so that you can see where the "ink" is being placed. You can also start and stop the flow of "ink" by touching the screen with your thumb and forefinger at the same time. This gives you more control over the placement of line work, which is very helpful when sketching on top of intricate floor plans. The application also lets you erase sketched line work incrementally by shaking the device. The screen shots at the beginning of Chapters IV and V are examples of the work the application produces.

User comments concerning the uSketchit+ application have focused on its inability to draw text for notes and its lack of background color options for sketching. Sketching the lettering for notes on the screen of a handheld device is extremely difficult if not impossible. A better way to place notes on sketched images is to save the sketch to the camera roll and open it in the uCantMeanIt application discussed below. This application lets users type the characters for notes using a keyboard and then place the text. Regarding the desire for colored backgrounds to sketch on, images with colored fields could be saved to the camera roll and opened in uSketchit+. Another option would be have an image of a grid in the camera roll, open it in the application and use it to guide the placement of sketched line work.

▶ uCantMeanIt ◀

I recall being on a project where we had some very complex, decorative column capitals. It was virtually impossible to describe the part of the decoration that needed to be corrected by using two dimensional shop drawings. If I had been able to take a picture of the condition, and then place a note on that image, I could have sent it to the contractor immediately. Instead, I had to go back to the office and try to generate a drawing that showed the condition. If I had had uCantMeanIt, I would have been able to deal with the issue after taking the photograph and placing the notes regarding the problem.

The name of this application is based on the idea that we can call up a picture of someone and place a bubble note above their head that could say anything, which of course they would not mean. But the application can also perform a useful function for design and construction professionals. Placing notes on mobile drawings or pictures of job conditions is now possible in the palm of your hand. After importing an image, the application presents a screen where you can type a note. This screen also lets you paste text from other applications like Dragon Dictation, which creates text from voice. This is particularly helpful when a note is long and involved and would take a considerable amount of time to type. The application then places a bubble on the image with your text and lets you move it into place by touching the screen. You then touch a point on the screen where the tip of the tail for the bubble note needs to occur. The user can add bubble notes with the "Add" button and delete bubble notes with the "Undo" button. You can be very accurate with the placement of the bubble note and the point where the note applies. The application is a mobile "sticky note" tool. The screen shots at the beginning of Chapters VI, VII, and VIII are examples of the work the application produces.

Comments on the uCantMeanIt application have centered on problems with the sequence of steps associated with the placing of bubble notes and "tails". It is important that users observe the "procedural hints" for producing and placing notes that appear and disappear. Each step gives users options for carefully placing notes within images and need to occur in the proper sequence. The process becomes very intuitive with practice.

▶ uPunchit+ ◀

Once I was going through the very cumbersome process of creating a punch list for a project that was close to completion. This involved carrying a set of half-size drawings, taking notes on the job site, taking them back to the office, rewriting them, and then getting them to the contractor. It's a very time-consuming task. If I had had uPunchit+, I could have produced an image of a floor plan for each room, touched the screen to place each number, and added a note while I was walking through the project. I could have then shared the image and the list of notes with the contractor via email on the spot and kept a copy on my own device for the record.

The production of punch lists at the end of a project has always been a very time consuming undertaking. uPunchit+ lets you import a drawing image, zoom and pan to a specific location with the image, note the job title and location within the project, and place numbers on the image that are linked to notes. The application simulates the use of tracing paper over an image by applying a yellow film that helps with the contrast of new and existing information. Clouds can also be placed on the image to highlight a location. The email that is produced by the application includes a PDF file with your project information, your numbers, your notes, and your screen image. This 8 ½ x 11 document can be emailed and printed on any team member's printer. The PDF file can be augmented with additional notes, if necessary, in Adobe Reader before it is printed or the text within the email can be copied and pasted to a spread sheet. uPunchit+ could be very helpful to Registered Accessibility Specialists when they produce a TAS (Texas Accessibility Standards) reviews at the end of a project and need to reference sections of the regulations. The screen shots at the beginning of chapter IX and the About the Author section are examples of the work the application produces.

User reviews for the uPunchit+ application have focused on the limited space that is available on the screen of the iPhone for numbers and clouds. The size of iPhone's screen does limit the amount of information that can be placed on an image but can be appropriate if small subsections of larger projects are identified and dealt with in a sequential manner. Citygraphs has plans to upgrade this application so that it will utilize the entire screen area of the iPad.

All of the applications discussed above import images that are stored on the iPhone's camera roll. These images are in a JPG or BMP format rather than in the popular PDF file format. The images in the camera roll that can be edited by these applications can extend beyond just those for drawings, to photographs of field conditions, and screen captures of documentation in other file formats. All of these different types of images can be kept in one place on the iPhone and can be managed and edited in the same way. Videos that demonstrate how to use these applications are available on Citygraphs website.

▶ Other Apps for Design and Construction ◀

There are many applications that can help design and construction professionals to be more productive. In addition to those already mentioned in previous chapters, some of the most popular for getting real work done are the following:

inchCALC+ (William Lipsey, $4.99): This easy-to-use application is for calculations in feet, inches, and fractions. It not only performs traditional adding and subtracting but also multiplies and divides decimal units in metric as well as English units.

Convert Units for Free (free from Thinking Drone, LLC): This is a very versatile application with a user friendly interface that converts dozens of different types of measurements, including length, area, volume, time, power, and so on.

iHandy Carpenter (iHandySoft, Inc., $1.99): This application has five handy tools that a construction professional would use every day on the job site: a plumb bob, a surface level, a bubble level bar, a steel protractor and a steel ruler.

AutoCAD WS (free from Autodesk): This application lets you view, edit and share DWG files on the screen of your mobile device. You can open DWG or DXF files you receive as email attachments, and annotate and revise them while you are away from the office.

iTeleport (JaaduvVNC for iPhone/iPad iTeleport LLC, $24.95): This application lets you access your desktop computer from anywhere via the screen of your iPad or iPhone, whether it be a few feet away or from the other side of the world. Your familiar desktop user interface can be made available on your mobile device. There are limitations with accessing some desktop or laptop computers that have "gone to sleep."

Save2PDF for iPhone (EuroSmartz Ltd, $6.99): This application will convert most file formats including Word, Excel, web pages and contacts, into a PDF file.

Print n Share (EuroSmartz Ltd, $8.99): This application prints from your mobile device to most wifi/wireless printers. It has the ability to print over 3G. It can print emails, photos, web pages, formatted messages, and supports most email account types.

Applications for handheld devices are having a significant impact on the ability of individuals and companies to be productive. Karen Kerrigan with the Small Business Entrepreneurship Council recently stated in an article titled "*Saving Time and Money Through Mobile Apps*" that with applications "entrepreneurs can spend more time on higher-value activities – like increasing revenue and innovation – rather than in the minutia of administrative tasks or other time-sapping activities." Increasing revenue and innovation is how economies emerge from recessions.

VIII.
Producing a Project Manual as an eBook

Placing specifications in the form of an eBook is an idea whose time has come. This idea will save design and construction professionals production costs and make it more convenient to access specifications information from any location using mobile devices. Creating eBooks will also allow us to reach the seemingly impossible goal of having a complete set of construction documents in the palm of our hand. An eBook along with our mobile drawings can now be accessed in a meeting, in the showroom, or in the field any time, anywhere. There is no longer any need to carry around bulky drawings or a thick copy of the specifications. All of the documents that are produced by our powerful production platforms back at the office can now be presented on our mobile presentation platforms in the field.

▶ Another New Skill ◀

Design and construction professionals have a wide variety of skills, and self-publishing has been added to the list. Design and construction professionals can now distribute construction specifications to mobile devices using the internet or the cloud. Distribution of these documents, rather than being a cumbersome and time-consuming process, could involve nothing more than simply directing team members to a button on the company's website.

An eBook is a text and image-based publication in a digital form that is produced with, published by, and readable on a computer or other digital device. It is a digital version of a paper book. eBooks can be published in a PDF file format or as an EPUB file. PDF eBooks are simple and straight forward to produce and can be read easily on handheld devices, but their file size can sometimes be enormous. Recent versions of Adobe Reader have extensive mark-up tools for augmenting the content of PDF files once they are produced. EPUB documents, on the other hand, can have interactive content and let users search, highlight, and bookmark sections. They do require special e-readers like Apple's iBook application. A set of construction specifications in this form could have links to product websites, videos, and additional documentation.

There are a number of technical issues associated with the production of an eBook but generally, the process would include the following:

1. Conversion of office spec section files to the desired eBook format
2. Review of the converted files to make sure formatting has been maintained
3. Uploading of the file to a location for distribution
4. Notification of team members that the document is available

It is customary to keep a separate file for each specification section, so all of the appropriate sections for a project would have to be combined into a single file. Printing a typical Microsoft Word file to a PDF device driver is straightforward, and there are a number of utilities and services that convert Word files to an EPUB document as well. Adobe has a powerful formatting program called InDesign that can produce EPUB files. Next, keeping the traditional CSI format for specifications can be checked with Adobe Reader for PDF files and Adobe Digital Editions for EPUB files. Uploading EPUB documents that can be read on the iPad or Kindle requires satisfying the requirements of those devices' manufacturers. These methods of distribution allow the author of the document to charge a fee and provide tools to track sales activity. PDF files can also be distributed via a company's website, loaded into a Dropbox directory or uploaded to Google Docs. Finally, notifying team members that the document is available involves nothing more than an email notification regarding the distribution method. Different degrees of control and security can be placed on distribution, with usernames and passwords. This process is well within the ability of a small office.

▶ Impact on the Process ◀

How does the distribution of specifications electronically compare with the traditional process of transmitting construction manuals to building contractors? The process has evolved from delivering

Word files to a reproduction company, and having them print copies of the spec book for contractors to the posting of the documents on an FTP or FTH site so that the contractor can download copies. Whether the contractor and his subcontractors pay for their copies or whether this expense belongs to the owner has always been an issue. These issues can still be controlled by distribution through a web site by using a credit card payment feature that is available through PayPal. Online credit card payment systems can also be used for the sale of other types of eBooks produced by a company. The transmission of information via paper, and all of the shipping and handling effort associated with it, is eliminated.

In addition to the ease of distribution via PDF files available on a website, there can be savings in time and money associated with the revision process. A specification commonly goes through multiple revisions. Each revision requires that the producer re-publish, re-print and re-distribute the section that has changed. With the self-publishing and distribution of specifications, the first, second, and subsequent editions can be discontinued and republished. Mobile drawings and specifications have made paper documents obsolete.

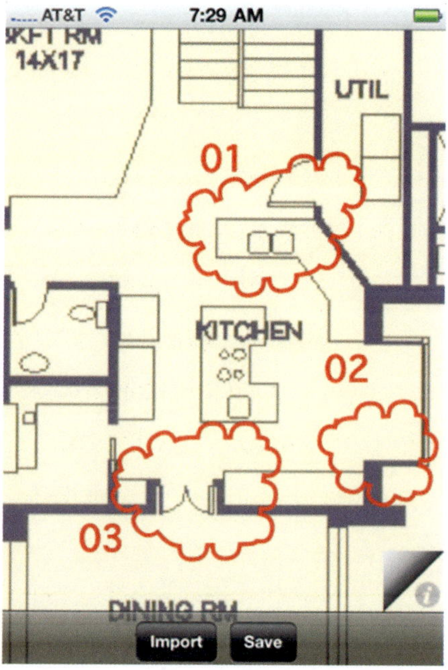

IX.
The Future of the Industry

Like most healthy organisms, the construction industry has changed, especially since the beginning of the recession that started in 2007. Dramatic downsizing is evident in all aspects of the industry. The goal of this book has been to recognize this event and deal with it by presenting ideas for how smaller teams and organizations can use current technology to produce more projects of better quality, faster, using fewer resources. We can make people more productive by integrating new, easy-to-use, inexpensive, and readily available technological tools into the way we produce projects.

▶ Changes in the Construction Industry ◀

Presently, most construction companies are small, with 68 percent of construction establishments employing fewer than five workers, according to the U.S. Bureau of Labor Statistics. The construction industry is also heavily populated with self-employed individuals and it is highly competitive. More companies are chasing fewer projects and the inevitable result will be a shakeout and consolidation of these companies. To stay competitive in the construction industry, individuals and companies need to be on the leading edge of technology and demonstrate this to customers. Using new tools can set a company apart. Smartphones and tablets do this by providing a new level of speed and mobility to the construction process. A forward-thinking company in the design and construction industry, even a small one, can demonstrate a new level of technical ability and a commitment to advancement by investing in these inexpensive devices. Smaller firms can gain a marketing and competitive advantage when they demonstrate skills with these tools.

Teams are getting bigger, however, and they are being spread out over larger distances. The need for specialized consultants who can deal with new, more complex systems and regulatory issues is growing. This increased sphere of influence for organizations requires closer communication and synchronization. The ability of handheld devices to communicate concepts quickly is the way to address this challenge. Construction activity is tied to the overall economy, and although the recession has technically ended, the recovery is sluggish, and the design and construction industry may not rebound for some time. This is an opportunity, however, to retool and rethink the way we do business.

▶ Construction in the Twenty-First Century ◀

Imagine walking around a job site in your hardhat, carrying an armful of drawings. Getting to the sheets, even if they are half-size, is difficult. Taking notes is next to impossible. Now imagine that your drawings, specifications, ASIs, RFIs and supplemental drawings are available in an electronic form and accessible on your smartphone or tablet. Now you can retrieve the documents you need by touching the screen. You can pan around a mobile drawing and zoom in on a detail by pinching the surface of the screen. You can sketch on these images, make notes on them as you walk the site, and share your work with the person next to you, or in an office a thousand miles away, via email with a few taps on the screen. All of this is made possible by carrying a battery powered mobile "wifi hotspot." Properly documenting conditions and decisions on a job site, in a meeting, or in a show room have always been critical. Now we have the tools to make this process more convenient.

This vision is now reality. The technology is available. Its implementation, however, calls for a change in the mindset within the industry. It's starting to happen. Construction related technology may not be as prevalent as what we see in the financial services industry, which lives and dies on technology, but it is coming. Young people will see to it.

The first wave of modern technology to hit the construction industry never made it out of the office. Created mainly for use by young technicians with project managers looking over their shoulders, early CAD systems were and still are, expensive and difficult to use. They were never meant for the field. Even more powerful and expensive office based BIM systems that require even more technical expertise and computing power are becoming the norm. The same limitation that has always been present with these systems is still there. Drawings, specifications, shop drawings, and other types of documentation still have to be printed and present in a paper form when on the job site.

What distinguishes today's emerging "mobile" construction technology from the first wave of "office" based technology is that it is user friendly. The devices, their applications, and the information that these tools produce are more available to more people. We can now have more decentralized specialists solving problems and dealing with unforeseen circumstances anytime, anywhere. Problems do not always happen during regular office hours.

Mobile technology opens up more lines of communication by bypassing the limitations created by paper documents. For the first time we have easy-to-use hardware that can present complex images clearly. We still need office-based *production* systems to produce construction documents, but now we have mobile *presentation* systems that can make them more accessible. It is not necessary that we be technical specialists to use these mobile tools. Individuals and small businesses with limited resources can use mobile technology and become productive quickly.

Documents created electronically should be shared and presented electronically. Thanks to our new document production systems, architectural and design drawings have an added measure of precision and accuracy, and thus their file sizes can be enormous. They are beyond the capacity of current mobile devices to load and unload quickly, but with compact PDF or JPG file formats, this is not an issue. Today, no one in the construction industry would be without a CAD system, and soon smartphones and tablets will become just as indispensible. We can do a better job of reconciling the unforeseen circumstances associated with conflicts between budget, time and quality if we have, in our pockets, the documentation associated with the problem.

What's the next step? There are so many exciting opportunities associated with using mobile technology. How might it affect the design and construction industry? Beyond making it feasible to eliminate paper documents in the field, we now have a way to present three-dimensional models on our handheld devices. Creating a movie of a condition in three dimensions, and then transmitting it to devices on the job site, can help explain the way materials come together far more efficiently than multiple plans, elevations, sections and details can. Taking pictures or creating movies of conditions at remote sites with our smartphones can also go a long way toward explaining to team members in the office issues that need to be addressed. The use of the iPhone's FaceTime feature, which allows live images created by one device to be viewed on another, can give people on the extended team a real-time view of an event or condition. Instead of static, two-dimensional images that have been the traditional means of communicating concepts, we may be on the verge of seeing a new form of communication; moving pictures of models or field conditions with dialogue that can be produced and shared quickly. All of these tools are available on smartphones and tablets now.

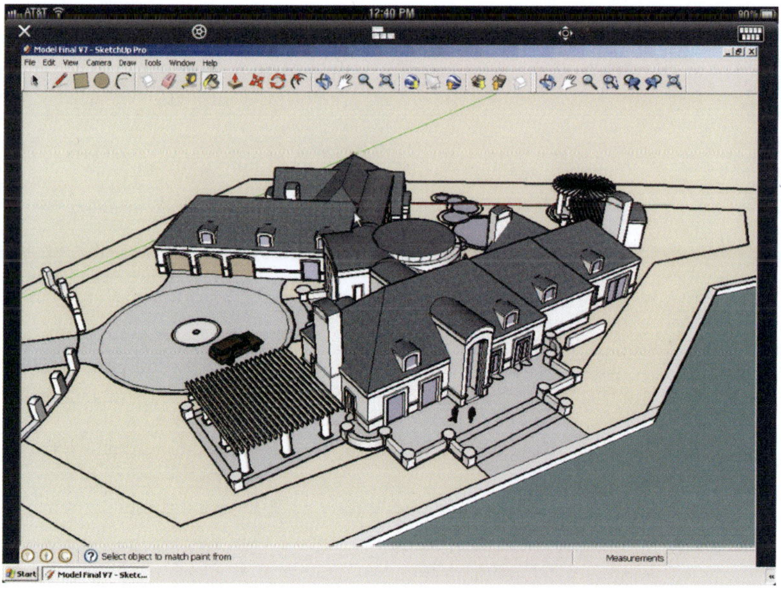

SketchUp Model in iTeleport on iPad

▶ Design Flow ◀

Design flow is the combination of mobile convenience and creativity. Ideas for solving problems happen anytime, anywhere. If we have mobile tools with us that allow us immediate access to pertinent documentation regarding an idea, and if we have a way to easily sketch or note our thoughts, we are better able to capture and test our inspirations and share them. The impact on our ability to solve problems could be significant. All of a sudden, the process of documenting a solution no longer stands in the way of producing it.

BIM, on the other hand, doesn't seem to be consistent with the idea of an immediate sharing of inspiration. The production of complex models by a few people on expensive, office-based systems requires a considerable amount of coordination and expertise. Three-dimensional views from these models, however, on the handheld devices of clients, designers and contractors could go a long way toward increasing design and construction collaboration. Producing a complex computer model helps identify system conflicts during the design process, but if views of the model can be produced as needed and shown to the people doing the work in the field, model building and model viewing becomes a more holistic process. Displaying a model or a portion of a model on the screen of the superintendent's tablet could go a long way toward helping everyone grasp and solve a problem. Model presentations are also being made popular by technology that produces three-dimensional models of existing facilities. Older nuclear facilities are using this approach for as-built documentation purposes rather than producing plans, elevations, and sections. Mobile tools can be used to extend the value of models and give team members a new, cost-effective way to visualize concepts and build a consensus.

▶ New Expectations ◀

We've seen something amazing happen with the new graduates that are entering the workforce. They have learned to communicate electronically almost to the exclusion of talking. They have become masters at using smartphones and social networking sites to communicate. They have new expectations, and unlike the last generation of managers in this industry, these newcomers expect to work in a technology-rich environment. We need to structure companies so that we can take advantage of the skills of these newcomers.

Newcomers are also much more aware of the issues associated with sustainability. The desire to save resources, do more with less, and support and promote renewable solutions to construction issues is a very real goal for them. What better way to make a new contribution to the field of sustainable building methods than to rethink the way construction documents are produced and distributed. The amount of energy and resources associated with the production and distribution of multiple sets of drawings and specifications for a project are considerable. What if we really integrated the use of mobile drawings and specifications eBooks into the way we produce projects? We could save all of the electrical power required to print, all of the fuel required to deliver, all of the ink and paper required to present, and all of the labor required to manage the paper documents that now take up so much space. Perhaps this suggestion will warrant more support and encouragement from the U.S. Green Building Council in the near future.

The smartphone industry is all about convergence – the combining of discoveries that come from the development and use of different systems. Standard PCs are getting smaller, with netbooks the latest form. At the same time, smartphones are getting smarter. It is inevitable that the two will converge, and the de facto standard will be a smartphone with a larger screen, a fully functioning operating system, and enough memory and cloud-based storage to function as a laptop. The result has been the tablet. With smartphones getting smarter, the market for productivity applications is going to grow. Smartphones, tablets and UMPCs (Ultra-Mobile PCs) will be used more often in everyone's business, and applications developers will create more powerful and more useful applications for them.

In developed countries, facilities managers and building owners are concentrating more on existing facilities, while emerging nations are seeing more new construction. In developed countries, we're seeing projects that call more for retrofitting and remodeling, and adapting existing facilities instead of building new ones. This may be the future of the construction industry in the developed world. Huge new construction projects still occur around the world, but in the United States, we are seeing smaller projects that focus more on reconditioning existing facilities as inventories of existing space are absorbed. The production of smaller projects profitably requires greater efficiency. Doing more with less, and saving resources with handheld devices, is good for business. But what becomes of all of the expertise associated with the production and management of large, complex projects that is now located in the developed world?

▶ "Bottling" and Exporting Experience ◀

Globalization, expanding spheres of influence and collaboration between stakeholders at far-flung locations, means a broader knowledge base. Different forms of expertise will become more accessible. Professionals in small rural communities will have the same access to different types of skills as professionals in Chicago, London, or Tokyo. With our new communications technology, a construction project in Thailand will have access to the knowhow of professionals anywhere in the world. The experience of design and construction professionals, no matter where they are, will be in demand. A vast inventory of expertise exists in developed countries, and an equally vast demand for this expertise exists in developing countries. The spread of mobile devices is going to continue, and professional skill based applications on these devices can be the vehicle for exporting our knowhow to the world.

Design and construction professionals have the skills to produce the applications that can satisfy this demand. Today's mobile applications, like those in Chapter VII, need to be created from the ground up and based on the experience of individuals familiar with their field. Producing an application is like producing a construction project. It involves concept development with the client, documentation, coordination of consultants, construction, testing, and delivery. Design and construction professionals are familiar with this process. We are problem solvers and can be players in the exciting new field of applications development. It's time to chart a new course.

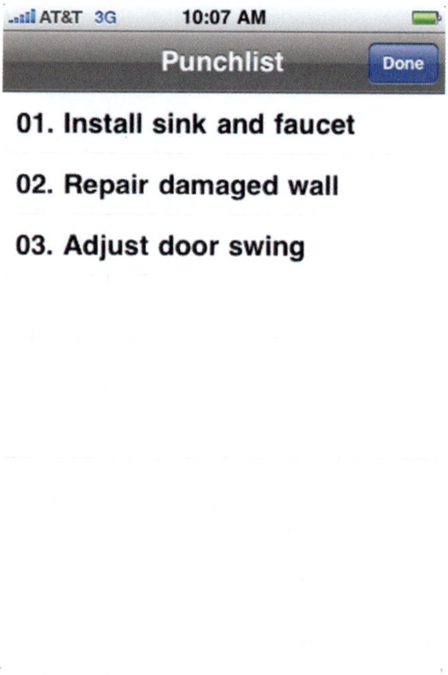

About the Author

Mr. Arnold graduated from the Georgia Institute of Technology in 1972 with a bachelor's degree in architecture. He became a registered architect in the state of Texas in 1976 and maintains National Council of Architectural Registration Boards certification. He is currently a member of the Texas Society of Architects and the Fort Worth Chapter of the American Institute of Architects.

Mr. Arnold has had a varied work history with architectural and engineering firms in Texas and Arkansas. He had his own four-person firm in the early

1980s. Mr. Arnold has been involved in the design and construction of a number of different building types throughout his career, including office buildings, large retail facilities, aerospace manufacturing facilities, distribution centers, churches, sports facilities, museums, and residential projects.

Mr. Arnold established Citygraphs in 2003. The company produced as-built electronic floor plans for property owners and provided a website and plan viewer that could access a data-base of these plans. In 2009 the company changed its focus to iPhone applications development for construction professionals. The company has also produced two consumer applications. CrowdSize uses Google Maps for estimating the number of people at outdoor public events, and ufoodieu is a social networking application for food lovers. Mr. Arnold is a registered iPhone and Android applications developer and can be reached at garnold@citygraphs.com

Index

Adobe Digital Editions........80
Adobe Photoshop Express.32
Adobe Reader.....36,72,79,80
AppShows.com..................60
AutoCad WS........................74

BIM (Building Information Modeling).............35,43,86
B2B (Business to Business)....28

CAD (Computer Aided Design)....14,16,35,74,86,88
Citygraphs........11,63,67,73,98
Cloud......18,19,23,38,40,78,93
Convert Units for Free.........74
CRM (Customer Relationship Management)..................6

Dragon Dictation...........10,70
Dropbox...............16,23,38,80

eBook...........39,40,77,78,81.92
EPUB............................78,79,80
Elance.com.........................28

FTH (File Transaction Hub)...............................15,17,81
FTP (File Transfer Protocol)...............................15,17,81
FaceTime.............................89
Flickr.................................19,36

Gmail.................................19
GoDaddy.com....................55
GoodReader.......................36
Google Docs..................17,80

Hotmail...............................19

iCloud.........................18,23,38
iHandy Carpenter...............74
inchCALC+..........................74
InDesign................................80
iPad...............9,38,40,47,57,64,73,74,80
iPhone......7,10,31,35,36,38,40,41,42,54,57,64,73,74,89,98
iTelePort...............................74
iTunes...................................38

JPG files...........23,35,37,73,88

Kindle...................................80

Movies.................................88

99Designs.com....................30

OtterBox..............................10

PDF files...........15,23,31,36,37,40,72,73,75,78,80,81,88
Picasa..................................36
Print n Share.........................75

Register.com........................55

SaaS (Software as a Service).......................................6,19
SDK (Software Developers Kit)...52
Save2PDF.............................75
Screen Capture.................23,31,36,37,64,73
Skype...................................29
Slideshare.com..................61
Sustainability.......................92

TAS (Texas Accessibility
Standards) 72

UL Connect............................41
UMPCs (Ultra Mobile PCs)....93

uCantMeanIt.............69,70,71
uPunchit+...................71,72,73
uScaleit+..........................65,66
uSketchit+..................67,68,69

Printed in Dunstable, United Kingdom

91231352R00065